U.S. HISTORY Need to Know

The Drafting of the Constitution

SilverTip

by Daniel R. Faust

Consultant: Caitlin Krieck
Social Studies Teacher and Instructional Coach
The Lab School of Washington

BEARPORT
PUBLISHING

Minneapolis, Minnesota

Credits
Cover and title page, © U.S. National Archives and Records Administration/Wikimedia Creative Commons license 3.0; 5, © Monkey Business Images/Shutterstock; 7, © Everett Collection/Shutterstock; 9, © f11photo/Shutterstock; 11, © Howard Chandler Christy/Wikimedia Creative Commons license 3.0; 13, © The Constitutional Convention/Wikimedia Creative Commons license 3.0; 15, © Mitchell Map Company/Wikimedia Creative Commons license 3.0; 17, © S.Borisov/Shutterstock; 19T, © mark reinstein/Shutterstock; 19M, © Alexandros Michailidis/Shutterstock; 19B, © Fred Schilling/Wikimedia Creative Commons license 3.0; 21, © MediaPunch Inc/Alamy; 23, © Ken Lund/Wikimedia Creative Commons license 3.0; 25, © rbpe24203100/Library of Congress; 26–27, © J. Helgason/Shutterstock; 28T, © LC-USZ62-59464/Library of Congress; 28ML, © Ken Lund/Wikimedia Creative Commons license 3.0; 28MR, © ungvar/Shutterstock; 28BL, © rbpe24203100/Library of Congress; and 28BR, © ungvar/Shutterstock.

Bearport Publishing Company Product Development Team
President: Jen Jenson; Director of Product Development: Spencer Brinker; Managing Editor: Allison Juda; Associate Editor: Naomi Reich; Associate Editor: Tiana Tran; Senior Designer: Colin O'Dea; Associate Designer: Elena Klinkner; Associate Designer: Kayla Eggert; Product Development Specialist: Anita Stasson

Library of Congress Cataloging-in-Publication Data is available at www.loc.gov or upon request from the publisher.

ISBN: 979-8-88822-033-7 (hardcover)
ISBN: 979-8-88822-224-9 (paperback)
ISBN: 979-8-88822-348-2 (ebook)

Copyright © 2024 Bearport Publishing Company. All rights reserved. No part of this publication may be reproduced in whole or in part, stored in any retrieval system, or transmitted in any form or by any means, electronic, mechanical, photocopying, recording, or otherwise, without written permission from the publisher.

For more information, write to Bearport Publishing, 5357 Penn Avenue South, Minneapolis, MN 55419.

Contents

Rules Are Everywhere 4
The First Try 6
What's Next? 10
Another Idea 14
Something Great 16
Divided Power 18
Getting Agreement 22
Always Changing 24

The Path of the Constitution 28
SilverTips for Success 29
Glossary 30
Read More 31
Learn More Online 31
Index 32
About the Author 32

Rules Are Everywhere

You raise your hand before you speak in class. That's because there are rules to make the classroom run smoothly. The United States government has rules, too. They can be found in the country's constitution. This important document created our government. It sets out how the country runs.

A constitution tells the basic laws or beliefs of a group. Many world governments have constitutions. Some social groups have constitutions, too.

The First Try

The United States became a country in 1776. Its **founders** wrote a set of rules for the new government. They were called the Articles of Confederation. The Articles gave state governments most of the country's power. But the **national** government soon ran out of money.

> The United States was fighting to leave Great Britain. That country was ruled by a king. People in the United States did not want a strong national government like the one they had just left.

ARTICLES

OF

CONFEDERATION

AND

PERPETUAL UNION

BETWEEN THE

STATES

OF

NEW-HAMPSHIRE, MASSACHUSETTS-BAY, RHODE-ISLAND AND PROVIDENCE PLANTATIONS, CONNECTICUT, NEW-YORK, NEW-JERSEY, PENNSYLVANIA, DELAWARE, MARYLAND, VIRGINIA, NORTH-CAROLINA, SOUTH-CAROLINA AND GEORGIA.

LANCASTER, (PENNSYLVANIA,) PRINTED:
BOSTON, RE-PRINTED BY JOHN GILL,
PRINTER TO THE GENERAL ASSEMBLY.
M,DCC,LXXVII.

Something had to be done. States sent **representatives** to Philadelphia, Pennsylvania. In May 1787, they held a meeting. It was called the Constitutional Convention. The representatives discussed the problems with the Articles of Confederation. They tried to figure out what to do.

There were 13 original states in the country. Only 12 sent representatives to the Constitutional Convention. Rhode Island thought the Articles of Confederation were good enough. They did not want to make changes.

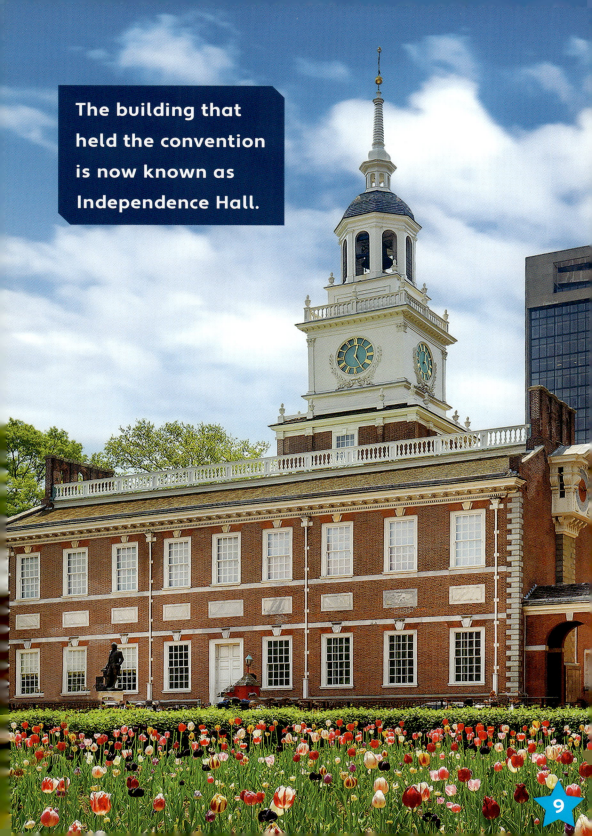
The building that held the convention is now known as Independence Hall.

What's Next?

The representatives realized they needed a new form of government. So, they started to write the United States Constitution. But what would the government look like? Many of the states wanted to keep the power they had under the Articles of Confederation. A few wanted a strong national government.

> Under the British government, the 13 states were colonies. They mostly ran their own governments. They kept much of this power when they became states under the Articles of Confederation.

James Madison had an idea. It was called the Virginia Plan. He wanted to make a **legislature**, or lawmaking body, with two parts. The number of people in a state would decide the number of votes in the legislature. So, the states with larger populations would have more votes.

Madison's plan also included other new ideas about government. He wanted someone like a president to make sure the country's laws were followed. Madison also suggested a system of courts.

Madison (*standing*) told others about his plan.

THE CONSTITUTIONAL CONVENTION · 1787

Another Idea

The representatives from smaller states did not like Madison's Virginia Plan. They said it would give larger states more power.

Their idea was called the New Jersey Plan. It had a legislature with a single part. The New Jersey plan gave each state only one vote.

> The New Jersey Plan is also known as the Small State Plan. The Virginia Plan is often called the Large State Plan. They are named for the types of states that supported them.

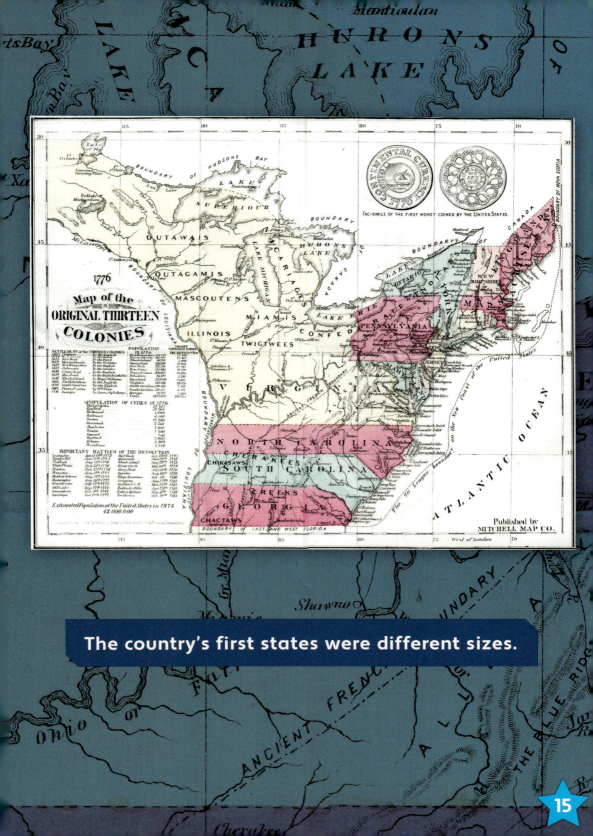

The country's first states were different sizes.

15

Something Great

After debate, the representatives reached an agreement. It was known as the Great **Compromise**. That's because it took parts from each plan. The compromise made a legislature with two parts, called houses. One was based on population. The other gave every state two votes.

> The legislature is called Congress. The two houses are called the House of Representatives and the Senate. For most laws, both houses need to agree.

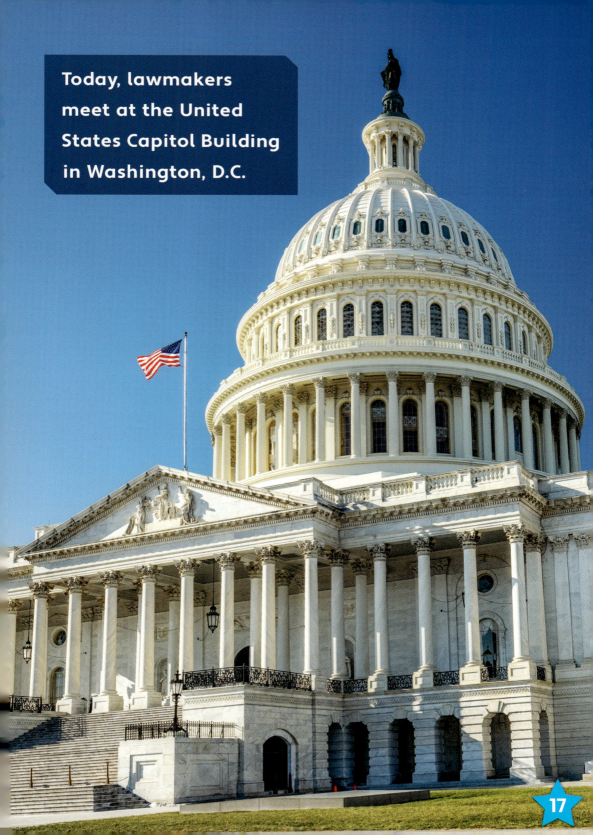

Today, lawmakers meet at the United States Capitol Building in Washington, D.C.

Divided Power

The Constitution also created a bigger, stronger national government. There were three branches. Each branch was given specific powers. The legislative branch was to make laws. The **executive** branch would make sure the laws were followed. The **judicial** branch decided if laws were fair.

> Many lawmakers work together in the legislative branch. The head of the executive branch is the president. The Supreme Court is at the top of the judicial branch.

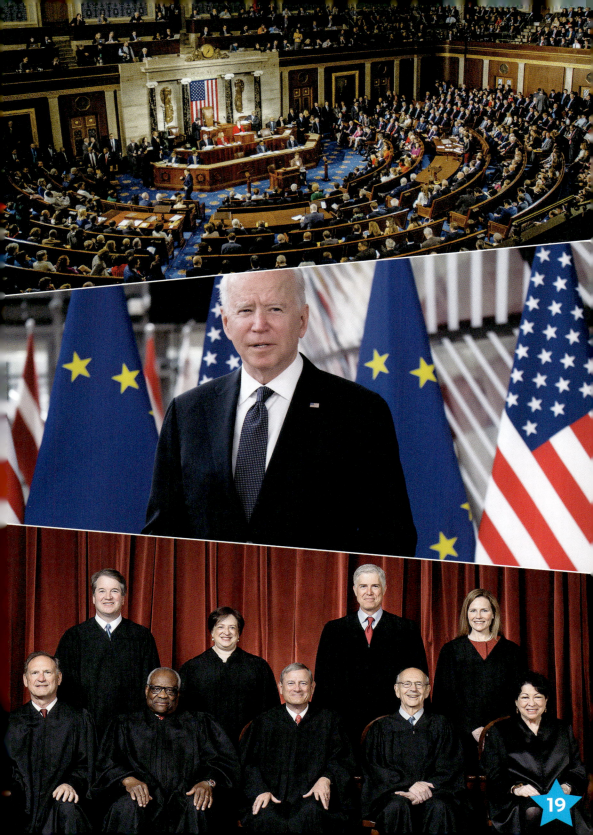

Power was divided between the branches. The writers of the Constitution didn't want any one branch to become too strong. So, they gave each limited powers.

They also made ways for the branches to stop one another. This meant all three branches needed to work together to run the country.

The legislative branch makes laws. But the president can refuse to sign them into action. This is called a veto. The courts can say laws are unfair and stop them.

President Donald Trump signs a law

21

Getting Agreement

Once the Constitution was written, the work wasn't over. The states still needed to approve the document. This process is called **ratification**.

At least nine states needed to agree to the Constitution before the new government could start. Delaware was the first state to approve it. New Hampshire was the ninth.

> Each state had its own meetings to vote on the Constitution. The document was printed in newspapers in many states so people could learn what they were deciding upon.

First
to Ratify
the Constitution
of the United States
Delaware

The Compass Rose
Dedicated 7 December 1988

Authorized by the
Delaware Heritage Commission
and the
134th General Assembly

Sculpture by
Molly Sanger Carpenter

Always Changing

The Constitution was ratified in 1788. But that didn't mean it couldn't be changed. In fact, the founders had a plan for that! Changes to the Constitution are called **amendments**.

Within a few years, there were 10 amendments. These are called the Bill of Rights. They protect people's freedoms.

> Over the years, even more amendments were added to the Constitution. There have been 27 such changes to the document, including the Bill of Rights.

A Bill of Rights

as provided in the Ten Original Amendments to

The Constitution of the United States
in force December 15, 1791.

Article I

Congress shall make no law respecting an establishment of religion, or prohibiting the free exercise thereof; or abridging the freedom of speech, or of the press; or the right of the people peaceably to assemble, and to petition the Government for a redress of grievances.

Article II

A well regulated Militia, being necessary to the security of a free State, the right of the people to keep and bear Arms, shall not be infringed.

Article III

No Soldier shall, in time of peace be quartered in any house, without the consent of the Owner, nor in time of war, but in a manner to be prescribed by law.

Article IV

The right of the people to be secure in their persons, houses, papers, and effects, against unreasonable searches and seizures, shall not be violated, and no Warrants shall issue, but upon probable cause, supported by Oath or affirmation, and particularly describing the place to be searched, and the persons or things to be seized.

Article V

No person shall be held to answer for a capital, or otherwise infamous crime, unless on a presentment or indictment of a Grand Jury, except in cases arising in the land or naval forces, or in the Militia, when in actual service in time of War or public danger; nor shall any person be subject for the same offence to be twice put in jeopardy of life or limb; nor shall be compelled in any Criminal Case to be a witness against himself, nor be deprived of life, liberty or property, without due process of law; nor shall private property be taken for public use, without just compensation.

Article VI

In all criminal prosecutions, the accused shall enjoy the right to a speedy and public trial, by an impartial jury of the State and district wherein the crime shall have been committed, which district shall have been previously ascertained by law, and to be informed of the nature and cause of the accusation; to be confronted with the witnesses against him; to have compulsory process for obtaining Witnesses in his favor, and to have the Assistance of Counsel for his defence.

Article VII

In Suits at common law, where the value in controversy shall exceed twenty dollars, the right of trial by jury shall be preserved, and no fact tried by a jury shall be otherwise re-examined in any Court of the United States, than according to the rules of the common law.

Article VIII

Excessive bail shall not be required, nor excessive fines imposed, nor cruel and unusual punishments inflicted.

Article IX

The enumeration in the Constitution, of certain rights, shall not be construed to deny or disparage others retained by the people.

Article X

The powers not delegated to the United States by the Constitution, nor prohibited by it to the States, are reserved to the States respectively, or to the people.

The Constitution is more than 200 years old. But it still gives us rules for how our government runs. Being able to change with the times has let the Constitution continue to reflect what the people want. This is one of the big reasons it is still in use today.

Any new laws made by the legislative branch need to follow the Constitution. Government officials are still elected based on the rules of the Constitution.

We the People of the United States

...insure domestic Tranquility, provide for the common defence, promote... and our Posterity, do ordain and establish this Constitution for the...

Article I

The Path of the Constitution

A lot has happened since the United States formed in 1776.

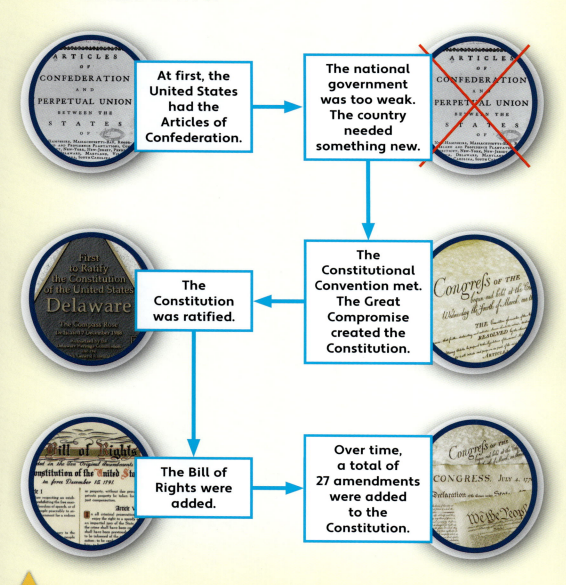

28

SilverTips for SUCCESS

★ SilverTips for REVIEW

Review what you've learned. Use the text to help you.

Define key terms

amendments
Bill of Rights
Great Compromise
New Jersey Plan
Virginia Plan

Check for understanding

What were people trying to avoid when first making the United States government?

Describe the main differences between the Virginia Plan and the New Jersey Plan.

Explain the roles of the three branches of government established in the Constitution.

Think deeper

How does the Constitution impact your daily life? Are there any amendments you think it needs?

★ SilverTips on TEST-TAKING

- **Make a study plan.** Ask your teacher what the test is going to cover. Then, set aside time to study a little bit every day.

- **Read all the questions carefully.** Be sure you know what is being asked.

- **Skip any questions** you don't know how to answer right away. Mark them and come back later if you have time.

Glossary

amendments additions, changes, or revisions to the Constitution

compromise to come to an agreement where both sides get something and give something up

executive related to the branch of government that includes the president and vice president

founders the people who created the country

judicial related to the branch of government that includes courts and judges

legislature the group of people with the power to make or change laws

national having to do with the whole country

ratification the act of officially approving something

representatives people who act or speak for a larger group

Read More

Harris, Beatrice. *The Constitutional Convention (A Look at U.S. History).* New York: Gareth Stevens Publishing, 2022.

Kenney, Karen Latchana. *Checks and Balances (U.S. Government: Need to Know).* Minneapolis: Bearport Publishing, 2022.

Taylor, Charlotte. *The Truth about the Constitutional Convention (The Truth about Early American History).* New York: Enslow Publishing, 2023.

Learn More Online

1. Go to **www.factsurfer.com** or scan the QR code below.
2. Enter "**Drafting Constitution**" into the search box.
3. Click on the cover of this book to see a list of websites.

Index

Articles of Confederation 6–8, 10, 28

Congress 16

Constitutional Convention 8–9, 28

executive 18

Great Compromise 16, 28

judicial 18

legislature 12, 14, 16, 18, 20, 26

Madison, James 12–14

New Jersey Plan 14

Philadelphia, PA 8

ratification 22, 24, 28

Supreme Court 18

veto 20

Virginia Plan 12, 14

About the Author

Daniel R. Faust is a freelance writer of fiction and nonfiction. He lives in Brooklyn, NY.